MAKING WITH MATERIALS

by
Robin Twiddy

BookLife
PUBLISHING

©2018
BookLife Publishing
King's Lynn
Norfolk PE30 4LS

All rights reserved.
Printed in Malaysia.

A catalogue record for this
book is available from the
British Library.

ISBN: 978–1–78637–354–0

Written by:
Robin Twiddy

Edited by:
John Wood

Designed by:
Jasmine Pointer

CONTENTS

Words that look like **this** can be found in the glossary on page 24.

WHAT ARE MATERIALS?

HAVE A LOOK AROUND YOU. CAN YOU SEE ANY MATERIALS?

What's it made of?

What's it made of?

What's it made of?

What's it made of?

What's it made of?

What's it made of?

Are you sitting in a chair? What is that chair made of? Metal? Plastic? Wood? These are all materials. Every object is made from different types of materials.

This book is made of paper. Your clothes are made of fabric. These are both types of material. Materials can be hard, soft, strong or weak. What other types of materials can you think of?

Materials can be found in nature, like wood, or made by people, like plastic.

WORKING WITH WOOD

DO YOU OWN ANYTHING THAT IS MADE OF WOOD?

Wood is made from trees. People who make things with wood are called carpenters. Carpenters use special tools to cut, shape and stick wood together.

Hammer

Saw

Nails

Tape Measure

Hand Plane

Drill

Chisel

This house is new but people have been using wood to build with for over 10,000 years!

Wood is used to make lots of things, such as houses, furniture and boats. Wood from different trees has different **properties**. Some wood is very hard and some is soft. Wood also floats in water.

GLAZING WITH GLASS

Glass is a really useful material. Its special property is that it is **transparent**. It is used for making windows, mirrors, screens, and much more.

Glass is really useful, but how is it made? Believe it or not, glass is actually made from sand. The sand is heated up until it becomes a liquid. When it cools, it has changed into glass.

When the glass begins to cool, it can be shaped.

PLAYING WITH PAPER

HOW DOES A TREE BECOME A BOOK?

Wood is often used to make paper. To do this, **raw** wood is crushed into small pieces and boiled in water. This makes a kind of wood soup called pulp, which is squeezed flat and dried.

Paper has been made from lots of different things, like rice, wood and even elephant poo!

Paper is made in a special factory called a papermill.
Papermills use recycled paper mixed with wood pulp.
It is very important to recycle old paper.

PUTTING TOGETHER PLASTIC

WHY ARE SO MANY THINGS MADE FROM PLASTIC?

This plastic is being **moulded** into a bottle.

Plastic is an artificial material. This means that it is made by people. Because it can be moulded into any shape, it has become a useful material in **manufacturing**.

However, there are some problems with plastic. Unlike wood and other natural materials, plastic takes a long time to break down in nature, so it is important that we recycle plastic.

Read more about recycling on page 22.

MAKING WITH METAL

DID YOU KNOW THAT METAL IS FOUND UNDERGROUND?

Copper was the first metal used by humans to make tools and weapons. People then discovered stronger metals like bronze and steel. Metal needs to be **refined** before we can use it.

Cars and buildings are often made using steel, a very hard metal.

There are still some blacksmiths today, although most metal work is done by machines now.

People who make things from metal are called blacksmiths. They heat the metal until it becomes soft, and then they **forge** it into different shapes by hitting it with a hammer.

15

FUN WITH FABRIC

WOULD YOU WEAR METAL UNDERWEAR?

Fabrics are used to make blankets, clothes, tents, flags, cuddly toys and lots of other brilliant things. Fabrics can be made from lots of different raw materials such as animal hair or plant **fibres**.

Cotton is made from a fibre that grows on the cotton plant. The fibre is turned into a thread which is woven into cotton. The coats of animals like sheep can be collected and spun into wool.

Cotton Plant

ART MATERIALS

WHAT MATERIALS DO YOU USE TO MAKE ART?

When we think of art, we often think of paintings. Painters use a fabric called canvas stretched over a wooden frame to paint on, but the paint itself is also a material.

Art can be made with anything. Some artists use materials they've found to make art. Some use natural stone or clay to make sculptures. Anything used to make art is a material. What have you used to make art with?

USING THE RIGHT MATERIAL

A chocolate tea pot would melt with hot tea inside.

It's very important to use the right materials. Some objects can be made out of different materials such as a spoon, which can be made from wood, plastic or metal. But you probably wouldn't want a spoon made out of fabric.

All materials have properties. Cotton is soft, metal is hard and glass is see-through. Both glass and water share the property of being transparent, but glass makes a better window because it is solid.

A property of fabric is that it is **flexible**.

RECYCLING

WHAT MATERIALS CAN BE RECYCLED?

Plastic Recycling Plant

Recycling means to use a material again. Old paper can be pulped and used to make new paper, and some plastics can be melted down and used to make new plastic objects. Recycling means that we can reuse something instead of sending it to a **landfill**.

Check with your parents or carer which materials can be recycled. Instead of using a recycling plant, you can upcycle. This means using an old unwanted object for a new purpose.

These upcycled shoes are now plant pots.

GLOSSARY

fibres	a thin thread of natural material
flexible	easy to bend
forge	to shape metal by heating and hammering i
landfill	a place that waste is buried
manufacturing	making large quantities of something
moulded	made using a shaped mould
properties	physical qualities of a material
raw	natural materials found in nature
refined	to make pure by removing a substance or material
transparent	a material that lets light pass through it, causing it to be see-through

INDEX